Contents

6	INTRODUCTION
8	**DEFINING GRATITUDE**
10	1.1 – Defining Gratitude
11	1.2 – Gratitude is a State of Being
13	1.3 – Gratitude as an Emotion
17	**FINDING GRATITUDE IN SOCIETY**
19	2.1 – Gratitude in Today's Time
21	2.2 – Gratitude Inventory
23	**USING GRATITUDE IN YOUR RELATIONSHIPS**
26	3.1 – Communicating Gratitude
29	**THE POWER OF POSITIVE EMOTIONS AND GRATITUDE**
31	4.1 – Benefits of Gratitude
35	**MINDFULNESS MEDITATION AND GRATITUDE**
37	5.1 – Mindful Living Day-to-Day
37	5.2 – Mindfulness Practice Through Meditation
37	5.3 – Getting Started with Mindfulness Meditation
38	5.4 – Practicing Gratitude Meditation
41	**UNBALANCED GRATITUDE**
42	6.1 – Superficial Gratitude
43	6.2 – Obligatory Sarcastic Gratitude
43	6.3 – Re-establishing Balance
45	**HOW GRATITUDE EMPOWERS**
46	7.1 – Become More Optimistic
47	7.2 – Become More Energised
48	7.3 – Find Meaning in Life
49	7.4 – Become More Sociable
50	**HOW TO LEARN GRATITUDE**
53	8.1 – Have Realistic Expectations of Life
53	8.2 – Choose to be Unconditionally Grateful
53	8.3 – Accept that the Good comes with the Bad
53	8.4 – Optimism is Key, But be Action Oriented
55	**DEVELOPING GRATITUDE HABITS**
56	9.1 – Developing Habits
59	9.2 – Practice Giving
60	9.3 – Writing Gratitude
64	**CULTIVATING GRATITUDE IN YOUR LIFE**
65	10.1 – Gratitude Meditation Practice
66	10.2 – Gratitude Journal Practice
67	Monthly Gratitude Journal
72	10.3 – Gratitude Breathing
74	10.4 – Gratitude Reminders
74	10.5 – Family Gratitude Practice
76	10.6 – Gratitude Letter
76	10.6 – Thank-you notes
78	Action Plans

PRODUCTION BY
Sabistar Pty Ltd (AUS) and The Verity Leadership Institute

CONTACTS

SABISTAR
studio@sabistar.com
www.sabistar.com

To order more copies of My Gratitude Journal visit us online at:
THE VERITY LEADERSHIP INSTITUTE
www.verityleadership.com

Limits of Liability/Disclaimer Of Warranty

The publishers and authors of this booklet and all products related to this booklet have used their best efforts in creating this product. You do not have the right to give this book away, include it in any membership site, or offer it as a bonus! You may not sell this book unless granted permission or have become one of our authorised affiliates. Violators will be prosecuted to the full extent of the law.

DISCLAIMER

THIS BOOK HAS BEEN WRITTEN FOR INFORMATION PURPOSES ONLY. EVERY EFFORT HAS BEEN MADE TO MAKE THIS BOOK AS COMPLETE AND ACCURATE AS POSSIBLE. HOWEVER, THERE MAY BE MISTAKES IN TYPOGRAPHY OR CONTENT. ALSO, THIS BOOK PROVIDES INFORMATION ONLY UP TO THE PUBLISHING DATE. THEREFORE, THIS BOOK SHOULD BE USED AS A GUIDE - NOT AS THE ULTIMATE SOURCE.

THE PURPOSE OF THIS BOOK IS TO PRACTICE JOURNALING. THE AUTHOR AND THE PUBLISHER DO NOT WARRANT THAT THE INFORMATION CONTAINED IN THIS BOOK IS FULLY COMPLETE AND SHALL NOT BE RESPONSIBLE FOR ANY ERRORS OR OMISSIONS. THE AUTHOR AND PUBLISHER SHALL HAVE NEITHER LIABILITY NOR RESPONSIBILITY TO ANY PERSON OR ENTITY WITH RESPECT TO ANY LOSS OR DAMAGE CAUSED OR ALLEGED TO BE CAUSED DIRECTLY OR INDIRECTLY BY THIS BOOK.

The world today is full of uncertainties and challenges and the last thing that anyone wants to do is to say "thank you," when so much in the world appears to be so distressing. With the hardships, turmoil, difficulties and problems that people are facing these days, it really becomes even harder to see the good sides of the world. Things become so irrational and unpredictable. The world becomes so different. Being grateful in this very ungrateful world is really challenging.

However, although the world seems so difficult and things might not go the way you want it to be, there are still many things to be grateful for. No matter what happens in your life, if you don't have the attitude of gratitude, you will never be completely balanced. Discovering being grateful when things go wrong, when problems strike, when difficulties happen will make a huge difference in your life and the way you feel about life itself. Life is always better once you feel blessed no matter how difficult things may seem.

Gratitude in this context is seeing life as a great and wonderful gift. Once you feel great about the world and about your life, you will find a balance of real happiness and peace. When everything goes wrong, it is really hard to be in the state of gratitude, but if you remain thankful about those little blessings you have, your life will become happier. Mastering being grateful in this ungrateful world is something worth doing. Author, William Arthur Ward, once said, "Gratitude can transform common days into thanksgivings, turn routine jobs into joy, and change ordinary opportunities into blessings." Gratitude is the unique quality of being entirely thankful for what you have, as well as always being ready to appreciate and help others. Gratitude is one of the primary keys to living a happy and prosperous life. When you show gratitude for what you have, you are content with your life and positive about all that it has to offer.

If you feel a lack of gratitude in your life and are afraid that it may be creating a void, it is time for you to take action and learn how you can develop gratitude to live a happier existence. If you are currently in a difficult situation and think that it is impossible for you to be thankful, then it's time you learned how to cultivate gratitude and achieve greatness. With your determination and effort, you can quickly develop a sense of gratitude and become content with yourself and your life.

You can learn what gratitude is and all the benefits it can bring, if you're ready to improve your overall well-being and live a happily, then you can learn to cultivate gratitude and achieve greatness. Gratitude, like any skill, can be learned and you can develop habits of gratitude. Gratitude is a choice. You can learn how to attract gratitude and improve your relationships.

"Every time you say thank you an angel gets its wings"

UNKNOWN

"This is a wonderful day, I've never seen this one before"

MAYA ANGELOU

CHAPTER ONE
Defining Gratitude

1.1 - Defining Gratitude

Almost every day, we say thanks. We absent mindedly tell it to the grocery store checkout clerk and to the Barista at our local coffee shop but are these sincere expressions of gratitude, or merely a response we've been conditioned to give?

What exactly is gratitude?

Is it something different than saying "thanks," or is the "thanks" a component of gratitude?

As you will discover as you read through this guide, a simple "thanks" can have a powerful impact on both the person communicating their appreciation and the person receiving that appreciation. This is especially true when the genuine emotion of gratitude backs the word. The question then becomes, what exactly is gratitude?

The Roman philosopher, Cicero, described gratitude as the greatest of virtues and the parent of all others. It is the key that opens all doors and is the quality that makes us and keeps us young. This statement, spoken more than two thousand years ago, is quite compelling. It speaks of gratitude as a virtue or quality of being. Gratitude is just this and so much more.

Gratitude is also an emotion. It is something that we feel deep in our hearts. We can feel it toward others, when people are grateful to us, or when we see a person express gratitude toward another. As a sentiment or as an exchange between people, there is simplicity to being grateful. And yet, when trying to understand this simplicity, we can find a more complex meaning. Gratitude is an emotion, it is an experience, and it is a conscious choice for awareness.

Connections in your relationships are both strengthened and fostered with gratitude.

At its core, gratitude holds an experience of universal belonging. We can experience a real sense of overall well-being when we practice the intentional cultivation of gratitude in our lives.

Write down what gratitude means to you. Define it through the following framework:

I want to BE grateful for _____

I want to DO (something) _____(for)_____

I want to HAVE (the following result) _____

1.2 - Gratitude as a State of Being

Take a moment, shut your eyes and try to recall a time when you felt appreciated. Remember this event as if it were happening at this very moment.

What did you hear?	What did you feel?	What did you See?
List the sounds you heard	List the feelings at that moment?	Describe/List what you saw

What triggered the experience? (A smell, a sound, something you saw, a taste, or something you felt)

What were you thinking at that moment? (first thoughts)

_____
_____
_____
_____
_____
_____

What did you enjoy most about being appreciated?

_____
_____
_____
_____
_____
_____

What process brought about this particular moment for you to remember it today?

_____
_____
_____
_____
_____
_____

THERE ISN'T A SINGLE DEFINITION OF GRATITUDE. GRATITUDE HAS BEEN CONCEPTUALISED AND DEFINED IN THE CONTEXT OF ATTITUDES, EMOTIONS, MORALS, TRAITS, HABITS, AND EVEN COPING TECHNIQUES.

GRATITUDE IS WITHOUT A DOUBT, AN INCREDIBLY COMPLEX AND DYNAMIC EMOTION. IT IS A SKILL THAT CONTRIBUTES TO THE SATISFACTION IN RELATIONSHIPS AND HUMAN EXCELLENCE.

1.3 - Gratitude as an Emotion

In this context, we need to be sure to distinguish emotion from the mood. Emotion is about something or someone. It is about a personally significant circumstance or experience.

A mood, on the other hand, is not connected to any object and is not dependent on any one thing. By exploring gratitude in this way, we can see that it occurs in response to an action within the framework of a relationship. Something has been given by someone and received by someone else. This exchange helps to foster the emotion of gratitude.

What's your default? (to give, receive neither, or both?) - My default is context is:

_____
_____
_____
_____

Write down the context that you would like to explore, and why?

_____
_____
_____
_____
_____
_____
_____
_____
_____
_____
_____
_____
_____
_____

Gratitude is an empathic emotion, which means that in order to experience the emotion in exchange, the receiver needs to place himself in the position of the giver. A feeling of gratitude in response to the gift requires the recipient of the gift to sense the giver's positive intention. It is this recognition and empathic connection that provides the foundation for the emotional experience of gratitude in the interaction.

We can express gratitude for any number of reasons. We can be grateful for receiving personal benefits, such as advice from a mentor, or we can be grateful for material items, like a gift, our home, or a car. Gratitude can also be fostered through interpersonal fulfillment, such as getting a hug from a friend. Or, we can experience gratitude for a monetary gain, like getting a raise at work.

JOURNAL PROMPTS

The use of prompts is optional. Feel free to write about anything for which you are grateful.

- Someone whose company I enjoy...
- The best part about today...
- A reason to be excited for the future...
- A valuable lesson I've learned...
- Someone whom I admire...
- Something beautiful I saw...
- A fun experience I had...
- An act of kindness I witnessed or received...
- Someone I can always rely on...
- Something I can be proud of...
- An unexpected good thing that happened...
- An experience I feel lucky to have had...

QUICK DAILY JOURNAL

Before you begin your day, list 10 things that you are grateful for?

What 3 challenges or obstacles can you learn from?

List 5 people that you are grateful for today

Draw a quick picture of anything that represented the best part of your day and focus on it for 5 minutes before bed.

"Feeling gratitude and not expressing it is like wrapping a present and not giving it."

WILLIAM ARTHUR WARD

CHAPTER TWO
Finding Gratitude in Society

When we look at previous civilisations, we see rich and powerful nations that are admired and respected. Many of whom had a culture of giving and receiving. Having that culture is what makes people strive to achieve their dreams. Unfortunately we live in an age where people tend to take more than they give or need.

Gratitude can be small or large. It may be as simple as allowing someone to cut in front of you in a queue. Are you being grateful for that moment or is it something that does not even register on your radar? Are you grateful for the small things in life?

Learn to adapt and survive by including small measurements of gratitude into your daily routine

As these civilisations grew people began to shift taking their cultures with them. Immigrants all over the world understand that hard work is the only way to forge ahead and succeed. When you have to leave your home and all that you know, you develop a new appreciation for everything that your life senses. You learn to express gratitude for what you have been given.

It is gratitude for the simple gifts of life, like a roof over your head and food on the table, which allow you to progress in the best possible way.

As proven by those that came before us, gratitude can play a seminal role in shaping your destiny and your life.

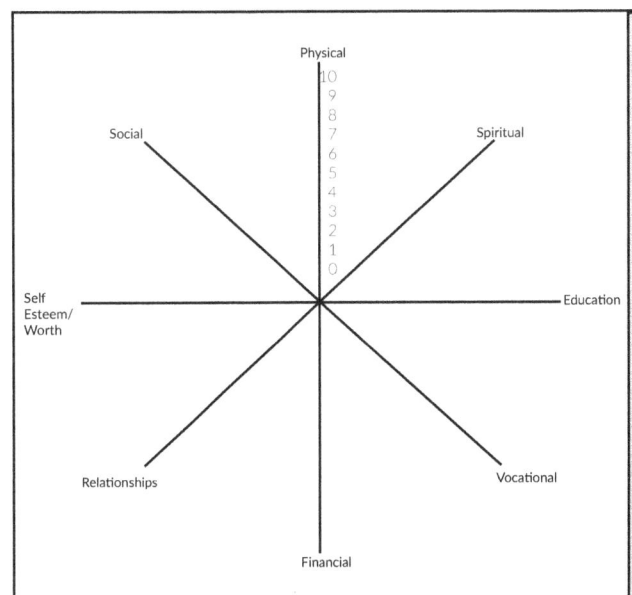

The Life Radial

The life radial helps you to visually map where you see yourself in life at the moment. It shows you where you are imbalanced at a glance according to your perceptions. When you know where you are you can work on what needs to shift. Use the scale of 0 -10. Zero being the least and 10 being the most amount of love or gratitude you have for these areas of life. Do this once a month.

2.1 - Gratitude in Today's Time

In today's highly consumerist society, where quarterly growth figures have become a measure of a nation's standing or where possessing a killer instinct is considered a great asset, the question then becomes whether or not gratitude has a place in our society.

While we are all still pursuing happiness, our ways of finding it varies. For some, we try to obtain it through service and charity, while others try to find it in esoteric books and at the feet of gurus. Unfortunately, for the majority of us, we try to find happiness through material acquisition. This has turned the society into one that feels it is entitled to all it receives and obtains, and shuns the idea of expressing gratitude for all that we have. Things are now viewed, by many, through the prism of sales and purchase, and some even view both relationships and possessions from a use-and-discard perspective.

Thankfully, gratitude is just as contagious as materialism. As soon as you realise that gratitude can help you reach the happiness and greatness you've been chasing.

What are you grateful for? List all the things that you are grateful for in your life. Think Spiritual, Mental, Social, Financial, Vocational, Physical, Health, Familial.

Have you taken some things for granted? List them below. How can you transform them into grateful states.

_____
_____
_____
_____
_____
_____
_____
_____
_____
_____
_____
_____
_____
_____
_____
_____
_____

Get yourself a charm bracelet and choose charms or trinkets that are meaningful to you. For example, you could have the following charms:

- A heart to symbolise your significant other;
- Figurines to represent different family members;
- An apple to represent health;
- A dollar sign to symbolise financial serenity;
- A charm that represents your current profession; and
- A charm that makes you laugh to represent humour and joy.

Each time that you see your charm bracelet you'll be reminded of how much you have to be grateful for. If jewellery is not your thing then consider another from of reminder like printing out a sign that you can stick up above your desk. So whenever you gaze at it you are reminded of the power of gratitude.

2.2 - Gratitude Inventory

Create a list of 100 things that you are grateful for. Divide your list into categories such as assets (things you have) people (relationships with friends and family), qualities (character traits and behaviours) and finally experiences (travel you have done or activities you have experienced), etc. Remember it can be as simple as something you love to wear.

"Gratitude turns what we have into enough, and more. It turns denial into acceptance, chaos into order, confusion into clarity...it makes sense of our past, brings peace for today, and creates a vision for tomorrow."

MELODY BEATTIE

CHAPTER THREE

Using Gratitude in Your Relationships

It is easy to get caught up in the hectic routine of everyday living and forget to express your appreciation to those that matter to you the most. Take a moment to think about the relationships in your life and consider a time when you felt gratitude for that person. One of the most common mistakes we can make in our relationships is the error of assumption. This occurs when we assume that someone in our life knows what we are thinking or feeling, or when we believe that someone else should know what we are thinking or feeling. The problem with this is that if we don't let those people in our lives that are important to us know that they matter, they don't know that they matter.

Name the people that you feel you need to show gratitude to?

___

How will you express gratitude to the people listed above?

___

Most of us have stopped being consciously aware in our lives. We have turned on the autopilot and are merely drifting through life. Our brains and body have become so familiar with our routine that we put little thought or attention into our daily lives. Our minds are usually so busy making lists, recalling events of the day, or thinking ahead, that we've stopped being consciously aware. We tend to go through the emotions that we know so well and miss out on all the nuances of the experience in the process.

What steps will you take to become more consciously aware of observing gratitude?

3.1 - Communicating Gratitude

Having an increasing awareness of gratitude can have a ripple effect throughout your relationships. There is evidence that when we share our gratitude, whether, in kindness, words, or gifts, we nurture our relationships, helping them to grow stronger and closer. Knowing this makes perfect sense and we need to explore how we can convey our appreciation to those that matter to us the most.

While there is nothing wrong with expressing your gratitude by saying, "thanks a lot," or "nice work," these expressions of gratitude are often taken for granted and seldom convey the message as powerfully as we want. One way you can verbally to express your appreciation in a manner that will foster connection in your relationships is by including three things in your expression: (1) observation, (2) feeling, and (3) need.

In sharing your observation, you just state what you observe, like holding the door open, washing the dishes, or taking out the trash. These everyday actions do make a difference, but they often go unacknowledged. Sometimes just letting someone know that you noticed can make a world of difference to that person. Next, you need to let that person know that what they did had and continues to have a positive impact on you.

The final aspect of communicating gratitude is often times the trickiest. It can be difficult to acknowledge that we need others, but we do. It is important to remember that we don't exist in little bubbles and that we are consistently affected by those around us. Letting someone know that they were there when you needed them is an open doorway to establishing a connection with others.

When it comes to thinking about your own relationships and opportunities for gratitude, don't limit your expressions of gratitude to the things that people give you or do for you. Sometimes it is just as valuable to share your appreciation for who they are as a person. Let the people in your life know that you not only appreciate what they do for you but who they are as well. Take the time to comment on someone's generosity, thoughtfulness, and compassion, or by just acknowledging who they are, and see how much happier you become in your relationships.

What steps will you take to show appreciation for the people and relationships you have in your life? (Share what you observe.)

"Gratitude is a currency that we can mint for ourselves, and spend without fear of bankruptcy."

FRED DE WITT VAN AMBURGH

CHAPTER **FOUR**

The Power of Positive Emotions and Gratitude

Wanting to be happy isn't an unrealistic desire. However, we seem to be misinformed about what happiness is. At times, we may think that we can find happiness in a new computer, a new shirt, or a new car. Other times, we may believe that indulging our impulses will make us happy. While these things in and of themselves aren't bad, you need to consider if any of these things have brought you true, lasting happiness.

Studies have demonstrated that approximately 50 percent of happiness levels are based on genetics. This means that there is some predisposition to happiness, but it also means that half of our happiness isn't wired into our DNA. Another study determines that 10 percent of our happiness is determined by our life circumstances like wealth, relationship status, health, etc. This means that if 50 percent of our happiness can be attributed to genetic makeup and 10 percent to circumstances, that leaves 40 percent of our happiness up to us and our behaviour.

This 40 percent means that we have a significant say in how happy we are in our lives. It's not all up to chance, or someone else's whims or intentions. We have a choice. So what does this have to do with gratitude? Well, it turns out that research has shown that grateful people are indeed happier people. Gratitude can reduce the frequency and duration of depressive episodes, which makes a lot of sense because it is hard to feel bitterness, anger, envy, hostility, and resentment when you are feeling grateful. By its nature gratitude has the capability to block more negative and unpleasant emotions. When it comes to gratitude, it is essential for you to realise that the feelings you experience are valuable and that they all serve a purpose.

When you feel afraid, you may become anxious. This emotion puts your body in a state of alertness, so you're ready for anything and can grow in tune with your surroundings. Feeling anxious when you are walking down a poorly lit street at night, is an appropriate emotion and can help keep you safe. That same feeling of anxiety prior to speaking publicly can prompt you to prepare for the event, and help you to have an excellent presentation ready to go.

Emotions that are typically referred to as negative are merely more unpleasant to experience. Bitterness, sadness, guilt, regret, shame, envy, resentment, and anxiety are not necessarily bad, but they can be uncomfortable to experience, especially if you are experiencing them regularly. Your mind is somewhat programmed to focus on these emotions and give them more of your attention. This is because these are essential emotions in that they give you valuable information about yourself and how you are responding to your environment. Without these emotions, you wouldn't know if there was danger lurking around the corner, or if you are viewing something that is opposed to your moral and ethical views. These particular emotions can prompt you into taking action. The downside to these specific emotions is that you can quickly get stuck there, and you can begin to find yourself living in uncomfortable places. A deep pit of emotional turmoil.

Gratitude and other positive emotions don't discount the negative experience but can help you keep things in perspective and keep you from getting stuck in those negative emotions. Practising gratitude is one way to transform your experiences toward more positive emotions and improving your relationships. If you work with appreciation, you will begin to shift your experience toward the positive.

4.1 - Benefits of Gratitude

Gratitude has also been proven to increase our capacity for experiencing other positive emotions. Often, gratitude is described with the same feelings connected to it, like love, compassion, humility, comfort, passion, and confidence. Cultivating gratitude can be a direct way to enhance these other emotions in your life.

Another benefit of gratitude that has been supported by several studies is that grateful people are more resilient and resistant to stress. When you can find the ability to be thankful for the things you have in your life, you find yourself able to move through challenges and difficulties in your lifetime and time again. Gratitude helps us see our strength, open our hearts, and experience the fullness in our lives.

The good news is, you don't have to go through a crisis in order to find gratitude. Gratitude is an opportunity that is there waiting for you every day.

Gratitude can be learned. With practice, gratitude can be a choice, an intentional way of viewing the world. This is not to say that you should discount or make light of difficulties or painful experiences in your life, but you should choose not to let yourself become overwhelmed in these times, and find a way to see beyond them.

You can look with gratitude at what you learn about others and yourself when you're moving through hardships.

List 20 -50 benefits of having gratitude.

How do those benefits serve your highest values?

"We should certainly count our blessings, but we should also make our blessings count."

NEAL A. MAXWELL

CHAPTER FIVE

Mindfulness, Meditation, and Gratitude

It is amazing how often we adopt someone else's emotional story as our own. When we hear it and witness it often enough, we will begin to fall into those exact same patterns. Whether it's a habit and pattern of complaining, or of doing things in a specific way, to some degree we all pick up on the habits and behaviours of those closest to us. While this isn't necessarily a bad thing, it is something that we can benefit from being more aware of.

How can we recognise these patterns and "borrowed" patterns? How do we move from the less effective patterns and move to cultivate an attitude of gratitude? There are many ways that you can progress toward this, but to build awareness, the best path is through mindfulness practice. The simplest and the clearest definition of mindfulness is nothing more than "paying attention on purpose." Intentionally bringing your attention and your focus to the details and the experience of one chosen thing. You can be mindful of anything, your breath, the food you eat, or even vacuuming the floor. Being mindful merely noticing the experience of something as it is happening at the moment.

Practicing mindfulness can help to treat and prevent depression. Taking the time to focus your attention intentionally can change the imbalance of the chemical circuitry in your brain and help you to shift out of your negative thought patterns. Other research has discovered that mindful awareness practices can enhance the body's general functioning and promote healing, immune response, stress reactivity, and provide you with a general sense of physical well-being. You will also be able to improve your relationship with others when you practice mindfulness because it allows you to be better able to recognise non-verbal signals from others, but also acknowledge our part in the interaction.

Because our lives can get quite busy and hectic, we tend to go on autopilot and miss opportunities for connection and gratitude. Sometimes, we even miss what we are experiencing at the moment. Taking a few minutes every day to stop, slow down, settle our bodies, and actually pay attention to the moments can have a profound impact on how we feel about the day and what we did to fill it.

HANDY TIP

Have your phone or a notebook beside your bed and every night before you go to sleep list 5 things you are grateful for.

5.1 - Mindful Living Day-to-Day

Our thoughts, emotions, and behaviours are all connected. Each one feeds into the others and shapes our experiences with others and the world in which we live.

Practicing mindfulness helps us notice our experiences, our relationships, and our environment in a different context. With mindfulness practice, we can pay attention to our thoughts, behaviours, and emotions without judgment. When we are mindful, we begin to see our world and notice all the opportunities for gratitude that exist. Any daily routine, task, or errand can become an opportunity to practice mindfulness and gratitude. You can practice mindful gratitude anywhere at any time.

5.2 - Mindfulness Practice Through Meditation

If you are struggling to incorporate mindfulness into your daily life, you can use meditation to train your brain to do it automatically. Mindfulness can be cultivated through mindfulness meditation, which is a systematic method for focusing your attention. You can learn to meditate on your own, following instructions in books or through the help of videos and tapes.

Some types of meditation involve, primarily, concentration, like repeating a phrase or focusing on the sensation of breathing. This concentration allows the constant flow of thoughts that inevitably arise to come and go. Concentration meditation techniques, as well as other activities, can induce a relaxation response, which can help to reduce your body's response to stress.

5.3 - Getting Started with Mindfulness Meditation

Mindfulness meditation builds upon concentration practices. Once you establish concentration, you begin to observe the flow of your inner thoughts, emotions, and bodily sensations without judging them as either good or bad.

Then you start to open your mind and notice the external sensations around you such as sights, sounds, and touch that make up your moment-to-moment experience. The challenge in mindfulness meditation is to not latch onto any one particular idea, sensation, or emotion, or get caught up in thinking about the past or future. Instead, you should be watching what comes and goes in your mind to discover which mental habits produce a feeling of well-being or ones of suffering.

There are going to be times when you don't feel as though this process is at all relaxing. However, over time it will provide you a greater key to happiness and self-awareness as you become more and more comfortable with a broader range of experiences.

5.4 - Practicing Gratitude Mediation

Gratitude meditation is one of the most influential and rewarding exercises you can do. When you're able to develop an attitude of gratitude you can start feeling more contented with your life and accomplish true happiness. Gratitude can make you feel good, and meditation will help you to achieve a deep state of relaxation and contemplation.

Gratitude meditation can be incorporated together, or you can spend a few minutes at the beginning of your meditation session taking deep breaths while you think of all the things that you are grateful for in your life.

You can start your gratitude meditation practice by taking a few moments to do some deep breathing relaxation techniques. Start by breathing in through your nose. This will extend your abdomen and cause your diaphragm to pull air into the bottom of your lungs, which will provide your body with a healthy dose of oxygen, and helping you to become more relaxed. And then breath out expelling as much air as you can.

When you're ready, sit in a comfortable chair, one that is suitable for meditation, and close your eyes. Allow your muscles to begin to relax. Let go of your thoughts. When you feel relaxed and comfortable start to think about everything that you are grateful for in your life. The more that you are grateful for, the more you will receive. Choose to practice gratitude meditation or gratitude relaxation and breathing, on a regular basis to achieve balance.

BECOMING LIMITLESS
BREAKTHROUGH YOUR LIMITATIONS

Your 1 day self-empowerment workshop to create an unstoppable new version of yourself!
Everyone deserves to live the life of their dreams, now it's your turn!

Have any of these affected you...

You spent months or even years being held back by circumstances deemed out of your control?
You feel burnt out from putting everyone else first.
You are forced to work in a job that's killing your spirit.
You want to motivate your team but you're not getting performance and results.
The flame of the honeymoon phase is over in your relationship, how do you get it back?
Raising your standards to be more inspiring and powerful is your choice, you no longer want to live a mediocre existence.
Ignite the spark deep inside you thats crying out for more.
You appear to be repeating the same mistakes and having the recurring disputes.
You want to be an inspiration to your children, and those around you.
You are too tough with your personal self-talk
You feel unbalanced in daily situations in one or more areas of your life.
You dream of being fulfilled both at home and at work.
You are pessimistic and take uncharacteristic steps to sabotage your success
You procrastinate and miss out on opportunities
What you dream about appears to be unattainable or elusive
Do you feel that it is time to let go of the issues that are weighing you down?

Why do you need this?

Becoming Limitless is a profound cutting edge workshop that provides you with the tools and process to living life on your terms. This is an opportunity of mind mastery at a level that builds your personal strengths and brings clarity to uncovering the secrets of communication in relationships, family, socially and at work. The realisation of balancing perceptions and collapsing those issues that are causing distress or dis-ease is a transformational experience that gives you permission to create real change and become limitless in life and business.

What can you look forward to?

Realise a deeper level of understanding your goals, dreams and relationship patterns.
Feel revitalised with a renewed sense of purpose.
Know how to be persuasive and communicate mindfully for effective results without upsetting others.
Reclaim the passion and ignite the spark in your relationships.
Enjoy more authentic and inspiring conversations with like minded people.
Be a magnet for people who resonate with you and know when to say goodbye to those that don't.
Transform to a more meaningful relationship with your children and peers.
Master how to put your needs before anyone else's.
Discover a simple technique to process the uninspiring elements affecting your life.
Know what to say to close the next business deal
Define and refine intentions and know how to put them into action
Finally! Master how to become limitless without losing or changing yourself in one day!

BOOK NOW AT VERITYLEADERSHIP.COM/EVENTS

"I would maintain that thanks are the highest form of thought; and that gratitude is happiness doubled by wonder."

G.K. CHESTERTON

CHAPTER SIX
Unbalanced Gratitude

So far, you've discovered that gratitude has a number of positive attributes and benefits. You've learned that people who are grateful tend to be happier, healthier, and are more satisfied in and with their relationships. Gratitude opens us up to being able to connect with others and can help us through stressful situations and experiences. However, it is essential to understand that every light casts a shadow, and gratitude is no exception. It is entirely possible to experience, or at least express, something similar to gratitude without the benefits.

In order for gratitude to occur in your relationships, there has to be an exchange from one to another. There has to be a giver and a receiver, and there has to be an awareness of that exchange. When the awareness of the gift is not present, the exchange becomes unbalanced. This can result in either a missed opportunity for gratitude or even a false expression of gratitude. In some cases creating a feeling of bitterness and lack of sincerity.

Unbalanced gratitude, or unhealthy appreciation, occurs when there is a sense that one should be grateful, but the feeling isn't there. It's the thought of, "I know I should be grateful, but I can't help but feel (guilty, awkward, suspicious, resentful) or some other variation of a feeling that results in being uneasy.

6.1 - Superficial Gratitude

Superficial gratitude is one that is not genuine or from the heart. It occurs most frequently when there is public expectation or demand for acknowledgment. The best example of this is the yearly award shows that are aired on television. The words of gratitude are present, but the sentiment behind those words is non-existent.

The challenge with this kind of gratitude is that it seldom makes you feel good. It doesn't come with the added benefits of the other emotions that are so often associated with gratitude; emotions of joy, happiness, love, connection, and even hope. Instead, superficial expressions of gratitude are often associated with a feeling of anxiety and resentment.

You can also end up with superficial gratitude when there are too many people to thank, more for the reason of not wanting to exclude anyone. When there is a long list of thanks being recited without the connection to what is being acknowledged, the sense of appreciation becomes diluted and has less meaning.

There are many situations where you may feel pressured to offer thanks, even when you aren't feeling the emotion, which can lead you to another form of false gratitude.

6.2 - Obligatory Sarcastic Gratitude

Obligatory gratitude shares some similarities with superficial gratitude. There ends up being an overwhelming sense of "should" behind the expression of thanks, rather than a genuine feeling of appreciation. This kind of gratitude often occurs when you feel a need to say "thanks" for a kindness that was received, but one that wasn't wanted or needed. You may feel obligatory gratitude when you feel obligated to thank someone for a gift that you neither wanted or like, or when someone is doing something for you that you want to do on your own.

6.3 - Re-establishing Balance

Everyone, at one time or another, has experienced unbalanced gratitude. The critical thing to understand is that this is not true gratitude, whether this false gratitude is stemming from cultural expectations or an intention to be perceived as better than another. False gratitude is missing the essential elements of the components that are necessary for gratitude to blossom in your life. If you find yourself engaged in an exchange of unbalanced gratitude, it is up to you to look for ways to restore the balance.

What are your cultural or heritage derived expectations of giving and receiving gratitude?

_____

_____

_____

_____

_____

_____

_____

_____

_____

_____

_____

_____

_____

"As we express our gratitude, we must never forget that the highest appreciation is not to utter words but to live by them."

JOHN F. KENNEDY

CHAPTER SEVEN
How Gratitude Empowers

On a psychological level, practicing gratitude allows us to become happier, more positive, and more amenable to finding joy and pleasure in everything that we do. Showing gratitude for the things we have and those around us also has social advantages as well because we become more generous and compassionate in our dealing with the world.

Studies have shown that gratitude helps us on both psychological and physical levels. Physically, when we practice gratitude in our lives, it can help to boost our immunity levels, which in turn can lead to us living a more healthy and energetic life. This can help to reduce the likeliness that we will fall ill and allow us to live a more active life.

Gratitude can empower you to understand better that life is all about the moments lived rather than continually looking out for the good or bad moments. Gratitude teaches us to be grateful for all the moments that make up our lives.

For example, take the case of someone who has just been in a car accident that resulted in them being hospitalised with their leg in a cast. Now, instead of moping about how they would have to stay in the hospital for a couple of weeks, the person is grateful that their life was saved.

7.1 - Become More Optimistic

Gratitude can help you develop an optimistic and positive perspective about life, even with all of its ups and downs.

Living life with gratitude will enable you to understand and appreciate that taking the rough with the unruffled patience is the key to your happiness, contentment, and peace.

Instilling an attitude of gratitude in children from an early age will help them value the blessings they have, leading them away from the current plague of the sense of entitlement that affects so many today. It has become far too easy for children today to take what they have for granted.

This ingratitude ends up putting them on a path that is difficult for them to find peace and contentment, which could impact their ability of having meaningful relationships in their lives, both at work and at home.

7.2 - Become More Energised

Among the many beautiful ways that gratitude can empower your life is the way that it ends up energising your being. The very act of balancing your emotions can make you view your life with hope and optimism, and provides you with enthusiasm to give your best in everything that you do. Anybody and everybody has a need for this vital catalyst that can bring exciting wonder into your life.

Describe what gratitude feels like to you. What sound do you hear? What do you visualise?

_____
_____
_____
_____
_____
_____
_____
_____
_____
_____
_____
_____
_____
_____
_____
_____
_____
_____
_____
_____
_____

7.3 - Find Meaning in Life

Life is more than the relentless pursuit of material possessions and achieving goals. Having a sense of gratitude for what we have and wishing the best for everyone else puts us on the path of self-realisation. This allows contentment to be a constant part of life, which enables everyone to reach out to those who may need help.

List the ways you find meaning in life:

7.4 - Become More Sociable

People who practice gratitude have more positive energy and tend to be more popular because of their more pleasant and affable personalities. This can help you make more friends and have a deeper, more meaningful connection within your relationships. In general, grateful people are more helpful, more social, more trusting, and more appreciative.

Define and refine how you intend to be more socially grateful:

"Acknowledging the good that you already have in your life is the foundation for all abundance."

ECKHART TOLLE

CHAPTER EIGHT
How to Learn Gratitude

Thankfully, gratitude can be learnt. With the right application of practice and discipline, you can master an attitude of gratitude in your life. The thing about gratitude is that it may not be all that challenging for most people to express when things are going well. However, the moment a crisis occurs or an unhappy situation arises, people don't see much reason to be grateful. Many would rather complain about their lives. The thing about gratitude, however, is that it is nothing more than a state of mind. You can, if you want, find a reason to feel grateful even in the darkest of hours.

Think of your darkest hour. Reflect and list how it served you or others around you. How were you grateful for the learnings?

___

___

___

___

___

___

___

___

___

___

___

___

___

___

___

___

___

___

___

No matter how terrible things may seem to be, there is always something for you to be grateful for. The thing to remember is that we are all on this planet for a short period, and as long as we live and breathe, we have something to celebrate. If things have gone wrong, you have to remember that they can also get better.

When you take some time to observe the way grateful people conduct themselves, you will start to notice some commonalities in their behaviour.

8.1 - Have Realistic Expectations of Life

Life rarely happens in the way you expect. The best students in school don't necessarily do better in life. There are numerous instances where somebody less talented than you is able to land the job that you wanted, or who find more success than you. No one knows what sort of cards we will be dealt in life. When you are prepared for the surprises that life will inevitably throw at you, always believe you can find a silver lining and be grateful.

8.2 - Choose to be Unconditionally Grateful

When you put a prior condition on being happy you will likely never reach that happiness. If you covet a particular sports car, that's okay, but if you decide that you are going to be depressed until you get it, what would happen for example if it suddenly goes out of production?

People who readily show gratitude for whatever good they see in their lives, no matter how small it is, are those who find it rather easy to be happy because they are balanced. Unconditional gratitude is definitely one of the prerequisites for living a balanced life.

8.3 - Accept That the Good Comes With the Bad

People that can appreciate that the good comes with the bad will find that their hearts are grateful for the good in life while realising and understanding the fact that there will likely be a corresponding downside.

8.4 - Optimism is key, but be action orientated!

People who find it easy to express gratitude for the smallest bit of happiness don't get fazed by the changes in life. They are eternal optimists who just need the slightest glimmer of hope to be happy and content. For them, tomorrow is another day to take action.

List the 3 highest priority items that you need to be working on right now that you've taken for granted?

_____

_____

_____

_____

"The way to develop the best that is in a person is by appreciation and encouragement."

CHARLES SCHWAB

CHAPTER NINE
Developing Gratitude Habits

Gratitude is something that we have endless opportunities to feel each day. The challenge becomes not getting caught in the negativity bias in our brain. The negativity bias is our tendency to focus our attention on the more uncomfortable emotions such as fear, anxiety, anger, and sorrow. While these emotions are essential for us, because they prompt us to pay attention to things that may be threatening or dangerous, we shouldn't live in them or let them be the ones that rule our entire life experience.

With practice, you can develop new patterns of thinking and new ways to experience your life. Just like with a new diet or exercise, engaging in a new behaviour for one hour, one day, or one week, will create long-term sustainable change. It can quickly become a habit. Something that you do automatically.

No matter what your situation, there is always an opportunity for gratitude. Even the most frustrating experiences can offer you a chance to practice gratitude, but can also allow you to observe it and be influenced by its presence.

9.1 - Developing Habits

Any new behaviour or routine will take time to develop into a new habit. The first time you drive a car, everything is new and requires your full attention. When you begin a new fitness plan, it takes some effort and commitment. Over time, the newness becomes something that you just do. The process is seldom simple and often requires some support or encouragement.

Developing a habit of gratitude will require some attention and effort on your part. While shifting gratitude into a consistent practice does take effort, it is a worthwhile investment of your energy. Research has shown that in addition to increasing your awareness of the abundance already present in your life, practicing gratitude gives you a wide range of benefits including:

- Improved ability to manage daily stress
- Increased optimism about the future
- A heightened sense of community
- Increased resiliency to traumatic events
- A heightened sense of emotional well-being
- Increased physical activity
- Improved sleep
- Improved physical health
- Reduction in feelings of depression and feelings of anxiety
- Positive impact on both cardiovascular and immune functions

List possible behaviours you wish to form as habits:

_____
_____
_____
_____
_____
_____
_____
_____
_____
_____
_____
_____
_____
_____
_____
_____
_____
_____
_____
_____
_____
_____
_____
_____
_____

It is critical to remember that habits take time to develop. There may be days where you forget about gratitude altogether. That's alright. You can pick up the practice again the following day. Over time, the practice of gratitude will become more automatic. Just like learning anything new, you have to give yourself patience and time to develop gratitude habits. With continued practice, you will notice the rewards in your own life unfold.

Weekly Habit Forming Practice Chart

BEHAVIOUR YOU WANT	MON	TUE	WED	THU	FRI

9.2 - Practicing Giving

Entitled is a word that is used to describe many people today. Entitlement is one of the most significant obstacles to gratitude. When you believe that everything is owed to you, how can you feel grateful or genuinely appreciative? This belief of deserving creates a wall that blocks gratitude.

So, the question becomes how do you shift from an attitude of entitlement to one of gratitude? There are several ways that you can accomplish this. First, you can start by adjusting your own attitude and model a grateful attitude in your home. You can also teach your children about gratitude and giving rather than about deserving and recieving. The key to teaching gratitude is to engage in activities and interactions that are focused on sharing, giving, and connecting rather than doing something in order to get something back.

As much as we live in a world where we are conditioned to give thanks, often without awareness, we also live in an age of entitlement. More and more people are finding themselves disappointed because they are not receiving what they believe they deserve. Believing that the world owes you anything is a false premise and will only lead you to experience disappointment, strains in your relationships, and further resentment and frustration.

List the behaviours of entitlement that you would like to shift in you or someone else, eg a child or a relative.

9.3 - Writing Gratitude

As you look for ways to combat entitlement and foster gratitude in your life, you can look to the simple act of writing thank-you notes. Often, when people talk about writing thank you notes, they are taken back to when they were required to write obligatory thank you notes for graduations, birthdays, and weddings. In these situations, the writing of thank you notes can feel a bit daunting and can quickly become overwhelming. With many of these situations, the gifts that are purchased are out of a social obligation, and the thank you notes are also written from a place of social responsibility. While this may not be representative of sincere gratitude, it is a positive step in moving toward developing gratitude habits, because it is a way to acknowledge gifts received.

With that, you can go a step further and move past obligatory gratitude and into reflective gratitude. Reflective gratitude happens when you are able to step back from a situation, recall the event, and re-experience the emotions that occurred during that moment or span of time. Often, we don't realise the benefit that we're receiving from someone until after we have had time to reflect.

Thank you notes have a positive effect on those who receive them. Taking the time to reflect on the relationships you have developed, and the gifts that those relationships offer you can move you from a place of resentment or victimisation into feeling appreciative of the gifts that you have received. It can also provide you with the opportunity to reflect on how you have affected those around you.

Think of a time when your resentment could have been shifted to a more positive state of gratitude and appreciation. List the people you wish to write a thank you letter to below. Then Photocopy the following page and write a thank you note to each person for what you have learnt or can appreciate now that you view the situation differently. You don't have to send it to them if you don't want to, the process of gratitude will take its effect with the writing process.

_____
_____
_____
_____
_____

THANKSMATE

10

"Be thankful for what you have; you'll end up having more. If you concentrate on what you don't have, you will never ever have enough."

OPRAH WINFREY

CHAPTER TEN
Cultivating Gratitude in Your Life

Now is your chance to practice cultivating gratitude in your life. This can be done by yourself or with others. The trick is to practice. As with any new skill that you are learning, developing an attitude of gratitude is going to take time. By incorporating the following practices into your life daily, you will find that, over time, you will experience the world a little bit differently. You will now begin to see opportunities hiding in the most obvious places. You will notice richness in your relationships, and you will start to feel more connected to those around you.

Not all of these practices will be comfortable for you, and some might even make you feel a bit silly doing them. That's alright. Keep trying them. Some of these exercises will resonate with you, while others may not. The key to cultivating gratitude and achieving greatness is to keep practicing until it becomes intuitive.

The first few practices are meditations. As discussed in Chapter 5, meditation and mindfulness are essential aspects to finding gratitude in your daily life. If you aren't familiar with the practice of meditation, these exercises may be a bit challenging. If your thoughts begin to wander, or your mind goes into judgment and questioning mode, that's alright, merely redirect your attention to the practice at hand. It is essential that you be gentle with yourself. There is no right or wrong way to do these exercises.

Put things into perspective. Things do not always go your way. However, gratitude isn't an emotion that is reserved for those moments when you get what you want. When things go wrong you can use the power of gratitude to release some of the negative emotions that you may be feeling due to the failure or setback that you have just experienced.

After a negative situation put things in perspective by remembering that every difficulty carries within it the seeds of an equal or greater benefit. When faced with adversity, ask yourself the following questions:

- "What's good about _____?"
- "What can I learn from _____?"
- "How can I benefit from _____?"
- "Is there something about this situation/event/circumstance that I can be grateful for?"

10.1 - Your 7 Steps Gratitude Meditation

You need to begin this practice by sitting quietly in a comfortable chair. If you are comfortable with shutting your eyes, do so. If not, you can merely soften your gaze to the floor approximately three feet in front of you.

1. Quiet your mind and gently bring your attention and focus to your breathing.
2. Take a deep breath in through your nose and breathe into your lungs focusing on filling your heart with gratitude.
3. Visualise your heart radiating with a soft violet light.
4. With you your next breath, visualise the violet light combining with a soft pink light that also fills your heart. Keep breathing until this light fills you whole chest cavity.
5. Exhale through your mouth and visualise a soft blue light emerging from your chest cavity, and moving through your upper body as you gently expel your breath through your mouth
6. With each in-breath, say gently to yourself, "I am filled with gratitude." With each out breath, say to yourself, "I offer gratitude to the universe."
7. Continue this cycle for four minutes. When you have completed the time, slowly open your eyes, or raise them from the floor.

10.2 - Gratitude Journal Practice

For this exercise, keep this journal by your bedside. Each evening, prior to going to sleep, sit quietly and bring your attention to your breath, keeping your head relaxed.

If you are comfortable, close your eyes or soften your gaze at a fixed point on the ground about four feet in front of you.

Take a few deep breaths, paying attention to the inhale and exhale.

Think through the events of your day. Visualise those events as they occurred, be sure to pay close attention to moments that contained acts of kindness, laughter, or beauty. As you notice these occurrences, pay attention to how your body feels. Pay attention to the sensations that you are feeling. What kind of thoughts arise in your mind?

When you've completed reviewing your day, gently bring your attention back to your breath. Write down your observations in the journal.

Start noticing the things that occur each day for which you are grateful. These things can be big or small; it doesn't matter. The magnitude of what you are identifying isn't essential, but instead that you are noticing things that you can appreciate about the day. You may be grateful for a person, for opportunities that were presented to you, for a good cup of coffee or tea, or perhaps that the day has come to a close and you are now preparing to lie in your bed and rest your head on your favourite pillow.

Every night, before you go to sleep, write down the things that you were grateful for throughout your day. Again, these can be big or small; it doesn't matter. Write down at least three things every day and once a week, sit down and review your journal entries.

My
Monthly
Gratitude
Journal

A Reflective Exercise

The following pages will help guide you through the elements that you will need to compile your journal. Think of them as prompts for the experiences that you want to reflect on and embed the learnings into your journal practice as well as practicing the attitude of gratitude.

Date Started : ___/___/_____

Three things that I am grateful for today are:

MON

TUE

WED

THU

FRI

SAT

SUN

REVIEW

MY GRATITUDE JOURNAL

Date Started : ___/___/_____

Three things that I am grateful for today are:

MON	
TUE	
WED	
THU	
FRI	
SAT	
SUN	

REVIEW

MY GRATITUDE JOURNAL

Date Started : ___/___/____

Three things that I am grateful for today are:

MON

TUE

WED

THU

FRI

SAT

SUN

REVIEW

MY GRATITUDE JOURNAL

Date Started : ___/___/_____

Three things that I am grateful for today are:

MON

TUE

WED

THU

FRI

SAT

SUN

REVIEW

MY GRATITUDE JOURNAL

10.3 - Gratitude Breathing

Even in the busiest of days, there are small moments where you can practice gratitude. Take a moment, two or three times a day, to slow down and bring your full attention to your breathing.

Notice each breath. Observe every inhale and exhale, noticing that at that moment you don't have to do anything but breathe. Once your breath has your full attention, silently say the words "thank you" on each of the next five to eight exhalations as a gentle reminder that right now, at this moment, you're okay. These silent "thank you's" can serve as a quick reminder of the gift of your breath and how lucky you are to be alive.

Do this practice at least three times per week. In the columns on the right, each day note how many times you manage to achieve full attention to your breathing.

DILIGENCE, DIVERSITY & DIFFERENCE

Discovering your truth is a lifelong journey of defining and refining your abilities and competence. The more you self-develop the greater your influence grows. Knowing yourself is the key to influencing others and is a crucial step in living with authenticity.

Our programs are designed to build your leadership skill-set through interactive online programs, experiential learning and seminars designed to help you network with like-minded individuals on their journey to truly becoming limitless.

THE
VERITY
LEADERSHIP
INSTITUTE

www.verityleadership.com

Weekly Breathing Practice Chart

Note Your Mood	MON	TUE	WED	THU	FRI

10.4 - Gratitude Reminders

It is extremely easy to forget something, especially when you are trying to form a new habit. Placing visual reminders around your home or workspace can help you stay on track with your goals. Create your own reminders that will throughout the day prompt you to think about gratitude, or merely pause and reflect. Here are some ideas for your gratitude reminders.

- Carry a small stone in your pocket. When you notice the pebble, pause for a moment and reflect on gratitude.

- Place a note on your office wall, refrigerator at home, or bathroom mirror that says, "I am grateful."

- Set the alarm on your phone to go off one or more times a day as a cue to pause and reflect on gratitude.

- Schedule a five-minute "gratitude break" in your office calendar two or three times each week. Use the calendar reminder feature to help keep you on track.

- Have a "gratitude partner," someone with whom you check in with daily to help identify aspects of gratitude in the day.

10.5 - Family Gratitude Practice

You don't need to practice gratitude alone. Gratitude is after all about relationships and exchange. You can create an attitude of gratitude within your home as a family activity.

Keep a gratitude list for your family.

Place a whiteboard or sheet of paper on the refrigerator or some other easy-to-find location and have everyone in the family add to it daily. Things on the list can be big or small; it doesn't matter.

- Choose one day a week to share the list together at a shared meal.
- Create a new list each week.

Our Weekly Family Gratitude List

10.6 - Gratitude Letter

There is always an opportunity for you to express your appreciation and gratitude, even if years have passed. Reflecting on those who have helped you in the past or present, and writing this down, can be a powerful means of cultivating gratitude.

Think of someone in your life for whom you feel grateful, but haven't yet thanked. Write a letter to this person expressing your appreciation for them. Let them know how they have affected your life. If possible, deliver the letter in person and read it to them before giving it to them.

10.7 - Thank-you Notes

Like the gratitude letter, the thank-you note is a compelling expression of gratitude. It allows you, as the recipient, an opportunity to savour the gift/benefit, and allows the person who gave you something the opportunity to feel recognised and appreciated.

Keep a box of thank you notes around and get in the habit of writing thank you notes. Write them for the unexpected, for someone who said something kind to you or helped you out when you needed it. Or photocopy the one below and keep them handy to send whenever you feel grateful for something or someone.

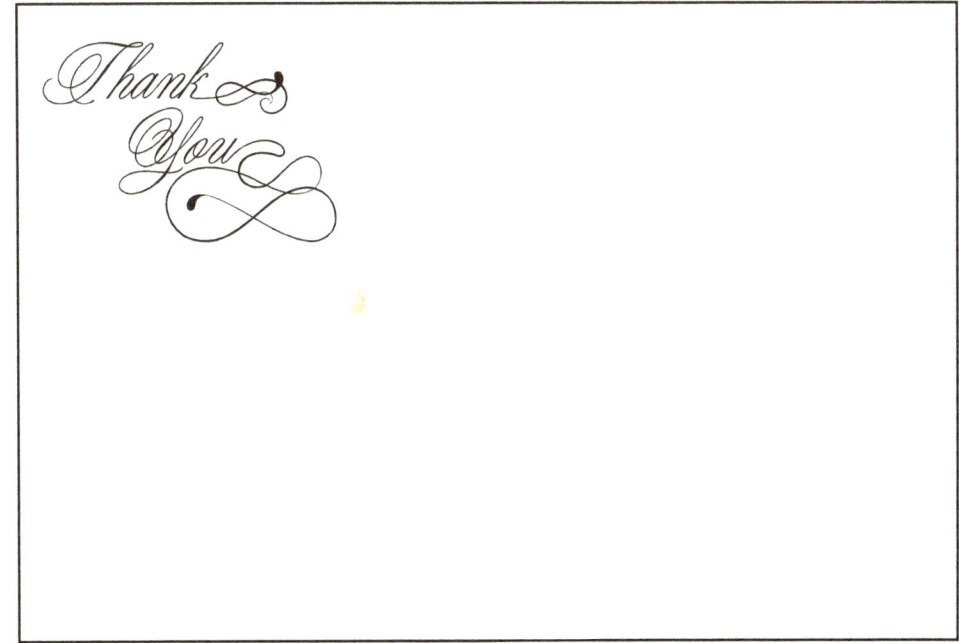

With Love and Gratitude

My Plan

List 3 objectives for your plan

1
2
3

Plan Type
Tick the plan you are working on

- ☐ **Enhancement Plan**
  Move a mission-critical skill from average to strength
- ☐ **Development Plan**
  Work on a weakness
- ☐ **Exposure Plan**
  Try out an untested skill to see where you stand
- ☐ **Re-align Plan**
  Get a plan back on track

Write down a quote that inspires you

My Before Description (Unskilled, Overused or Problem)

Some causes for me

My lessons

My Action Plan

Learn from Feedback	Develop-in-place assignments
Learn on my own	Learning from my roles or duties

My Plan
My After Description

My Plan
List 3 objectives for your plan

1

2

3

Write down a quote that inspires you to take action

Plan Type
Tick the plan you are working on

☐ Enhancement Plan
Move a mission-critical skill from average to strength

☐ Development Plan
Work on a weakness

☐ Exposure Plan
Try out an untested skill to see where you stand

☐ Re-align Plan
Get a plan back on track

My Before Description (Unskilled, Overused or Problem)

Some causes for me

My lessons

My Action Plan

Learn from Feedback	Develop-in-place assignments
Learn on my own	Learning from my roles or duties

MY GRATITUDE JOURNAL

My Plan
My After Description

My Plan
List 3 objectives for your plan

1

2

3

Write down a quote that inspires you to take action

Plan Type
Tick the plan you are working on

- [ ] **Enhancement Plan**
  Move a mission-critical skill from average to strength
- [ ] **Development Plan**
  Work on a weakness
- [ ] **Exposure Plan**
  Try out an untested skill to see where you stand
- [ ] **Re-align Plan**
  Get a plan back on track

My Before Description (Unskilled, Overused or Problem)

Some causes for me

My lessons

My Action Plan

Learn from Feedback	Develop-in-place assignments
Learn on my own	Learning from my roles or duties

MY GRATITUDE JOURNAL

My Plan
My After Description

My Plan

List 3 objectives for your plan

1

2

3

Write down a quote that inspires you to take action

Plan Type
Tick the plan you are working on

- ☐ **Enhancement Plan**
  Move a mission-critical skill from average to strength
- ☐ **Development Plan**
  Work on a weakness
- ☐ **Exposure Plan**
  Try out an untested skill to see where you stand
- ☐ **Re-align Plan**
  Get a plan back on track

My Before Description (Unskilled, Overused or Problem)

Some causes for me

My lessons

My Action Plan

Learn from Feedback	Develop-in-place assignments
Learn on my own	Learning from my roles or duties

MY GRATITUDE JOURNAL

My Plan
My After Description

Gratitude has the power to transform your life dramatically and is something that can be quickly learned. As you begin to notice the good that is surrounding your life and start to show gratitude for everything you have, you will begin to become balanced and more content with your life. Gratitude will allow you to become more hopeful for the future and excited to see what life has in store for you.

Start practicing an attitude of gratitude and start a fresh life, making it an integral part of your every day. Start benefiting both physically and mentally from the mighty act of gratitude. It is like holding the universe in the palm of your hand!

www.ingramcontent.com/pod-product-compliance
Lightning Source LLC
Chambersburg PA
CBHW031415040426
42444CB00005B/572